DEATH at DAWN

A Stage Play
by
Peter Mortimer

RED SQUIRREL

First published in the UK in 2014 by
Red Squirrel Press
Briery Hill Cottage
Stannington
Morpeth
NE61 6ES
www.redsquirrelpress.com
Reprinted 2014
Reprinted 2016

Red Squirrel Press is distributed by Central books Ltd.
and represented by Inpress ltd.
www.inpressbooks.co.uk

Cover by Dave Grey, Kimmerston.

Typeset by Brian Grogan.

A CIP catalogue record is available from the British Library.

ISBN: 978 1 906700 92 8

Printed by Ingram Lightning Source

THE REALITY OF A PLAY

THIS PLAY IS INFORMED BY THE REAL LIFE OF THE FIRST World War soldier William Hunter, but much of it is the author's own invention. Certain things *are* true and the following facts make their way into the play. William Hunter was a native of North Shields. Somewhere around the start of the Great War he joined the merchant navy and later jumped ship in Montreal. He joined up with the Loyal North Lancs Regiment where he served as a private in Northern France. In 1915 he deserted and was later captured. Hunter was imprisoned but escaped again. In his statement read to the court martial he said 'during this time I got in league with a young woman and I did not like to leave her.' He claimed to have been underage on signing up and it was the policy of the British Army not to execute soldiers in such circumstances. Leniency was recommended but this recommendation was overturned by Field Marshall Haig for reasons not explained.

Hunter did not speak at his court martial. He was shot in 1916 by members of his own battalion. The location was an abattoir. All the above are woven into the play's narrative, albeit the events have been somewhat condensed. Hunter's grave can be found at Maroc Cemetery, Mazingarve in France.

As a playwright, it was my job to find a possible motivation behind many of these facts and via that process create a piece of theatre which may have something relevant to say, while keeping its audience involved and entertained. Thus I invent a great deal as regards characters and development as the play attempts to find its own 'truth' built round the basic framework of William Hunter's life during this time. Like many plays the final product is an amalgam of historical events and invented character. I do use a section of actual transcript from Hunter's court martial, also the exact words of some of the officers' recommendations, but this is not a courtroom drama nor does it attempt to reproduce the trial on stage, which I suspect was fairly brief. The play also quotes directly from one of the letters sent by his mother Margaret to Hunter at the front.

The fact that later research revealed that Hunter was *not* underage when he signed up is incidental. It was the belief of the authorities at the time that was relevant. I feel grateful to William Hunter. He has allowed me to write a play based round his own tragic circumstances while feeding in the kind of personal concerns and interests which all writers carry with them as baggage. This is perfectly valid if the audience is convinced by what they see and hear. Throughout the writing I was aware of Hunter's presence, often he was at my shoulder. I imagined myself back at his age. Often I saw my son Dylan standing in his shoes. Writing the part of his mother was especially poignant.

There appears only one other instance of a WW1 soldier in the British Army being shot at dawn when believed to have volunteered underage; this was Abraham Beverstein of the Middlesex Regiment, who enlisted under the false name of Harris, possibly to hide the fact he was Jewish. He was shot for desertion on March 20, 1916 and is buried in Labourse Communal Cemetery.

In all more than 3000 soldiers were sentenced to death in the Great War but just over 300 were shot. It remains one of the most controversial aspects of the conflict. In 1930 this death penalty was abolished except for mutiny and treachery. The Second World War saw only four military executions. In 2006, The Armed Forces Act brought a general pardon for all those executed.

The forthcoming centenary has allowed a new examination of a war which has a grip on the nation's consciousness in a way no subsequent war has. Possibly because it was like nothing that had come before, nor anything that has happened since. But however great and important the theme, however historically momentous the backdrop, any piece of theatre struggles if it does not realise the importance of character. Thus for the last three years these characters have slowly evolved in my head, sometimes taking up more space than my everyday acquaintances. Let's hope they stick around awhile in yours.

I am extremely grateful to Alan Fidler and the splendid Tynemouth World War One Commemoration Project not only for offering me the chance to write this play (and the for the funding) but for the support throughout. Alan himself, whose knowledge of the war is encyclopaedic, fed me a constant supply of information while the project's active volunteers, based here at The Linskill Community Centre, North Shields unearthed a good deal of fascinating facts about Hunter and the subject area in general which they then passed on, making my own research demands so much easier. Many thanks also to Bill Griffiths from the WW1 Project. Bill and I worked closely and diligently on the practical challenges of making the play financially possible.

The play's cast is a mix of seven professional actors plus four North Tyneside drama students approximately the same age as Hunter when he was shot. In different ways, *Death at Dawn* has greatly influenced my recent years. Gestation has been slow, often painful, but this is often the reality for a playwright. The rest is now up to the actors and the director. And of course you, the audience – who are always the final arbiters.
Peter Mortimer
Cullercoats
Summer 2014

POST-SCRIPT
Like many, many others I was shocked and saddened at the death of our director Jackie Fielding in Spring 2015, aged only 47. This revival is in many ways an homage to her brilliant work on this and countless other productions staged in this region and elsewhere.
Cullercoats February 2016

DIRECTOR'S NOTES

JACKIE FIELDING, who directed the first production of *Death at Dawn* was a friend of mine. We worked together many times since I first met her in the early 2000s. I, like many others, couldn't quite believe it when she passed away last year aged just forty seven.

As I'm writing this I'm looking at a big, daft, red swivel chair that takes up half my living room and I can picture Jackie nestled in it after we'd gone out and got drunk one night for no particular reason, (or none that I can remember anyway). I really miss her not being around and I know of many, many people who feel the same. She did an awful lot of good in her life and I'll never forget her.

It was with those thoughts in mind that I agreed to direct the second outing of *Death at Dawn* after Peter Mortimer approached me and asked me if I'd like to take it on. We both agreed that if we were going to do it, we ought to do it the way Jackie did.

I had no interest whatsoever in "putting my own stamp on it" or any other such directorial/egotistical/ambitious nonsense – no – we'd do it the Jackie way! So armed with a DVD of the previous production and a copy of the prompt script this is what we are going to do.

I must admit, it's a first for me – I've never had to re-create another person's show before but we do have the same crew and most of the original cast so I'm more than hopeful we can pull it off.

So this one's for you Jackie. Rest in peace lovely. *X*

Neil Armstrong
February 2016

RECOMMENDED READING

The First World War has spawned more novels, plays, poems, films, music and documentaries than almost any subject in history. The more I read and saw, the more I realised how much more there was. Any book list will be arbitrary, but below are a few titles for those who want to look further into the subject of British military executions. With thanks to Alan Fidler.

Blindfold & Alone	Cathryn Corns &
	John Hughes-Wilson (Cassell)
For God's Sake Shoot Straight!	Leonard Sellers (Leo Cooper)
For the Sake of Example	Anthony Babington (Secker & Warburg)
Shot at Dawn	Julian Putkowski
	& Julian Sykes (Pen & Sword)
The Thin Yellow Line	William Moore (Leo Cooper)

If you are interested in the subject of soldiers signing up underage try:
Boy Soldiers of the Great War   Richard Van Emden (Headline)

PM

Rehearsal photographs by Dave Turnbull

CLOUD NINE THEATRE PRODUCTIONS PRESENT

DEATH AT DAWN
by
Peter Mortimer

Private William Hunter	*Stephen Gregory*
Private Jack White	*Dylan Mortimer*
Private Henry Stevens	*Jamie Brown*
Private Len Smiley	*Dean Logan*
Bella/Juliette/Claudette	*Heather Carroll*
Platoon Sergeant	*Pip Chamberlin*
Margaret Hunter	*Diane Legg*
Platoon Soldiers	*Alex Broadbent*
	James Gebbie
	Robert Wilson Baker
	Kyle Morley

The following characters are played by members of the company:
Recruiting Officer, Recruiting Sergeant, Ron Taylor, (Shields lad)
Montreal bar customers, Juliette's husband, Sailor Joe, Two Montreal Heavies,
Angela (a temptress) Capt. Barrett, Runner, three review officers.

Director	*Neil Armstrong*
Production manager	*Paul Aziz*
Designer	*Simon Henderson*
Deputy Stage Manager	*Chloe Ribbens*
Costume Supervisor	*Lou Duffy*
Hair	*Christopher Carr*
Lighting Designer	*Nick Rogerson*
Sound Designer	*Craig Spence*
'Drill Sergeant'	*Neil McGurk*
Admin	*Kate Wilde*
Schools Liaison	*Elaine Cusack*

The play takes place in North Shields, Montreal, Liverpool
and on the Western Front between 1914-1916

First produced at the Linskill Centre, North Shields, Sept. 2014.
This production opened Feb 19 2016 at The Memorial Hall, Wallsend;
then from Feb 26 at Discovery Museum, Newcastle

Funded by Arts Council England, North Tyneside Council and
Northumbria World War One Commemoration Project

With thanks to Customs House, Newcastle College, Meriel Johnston, Jam Jar Cinema
Kitty Fitzgerald; Photographs, Christopher Carr, Dave Turnbull.

SCENE ONE
(The Firing Squad)

> (DRUMS. HUNTER IS WALKED ON BY TWO
> SOLDIERS AND TIED TO THE STAKE. EXIT
> SOLDIERS ENTER FIRING SQUAD. WHICH
> INCLUDES WHITE, SMILEY AND STEVENS.
> BLINDFOLD IS PUT ON HIM. SMILEY IS
> SUFFERING FROM SHELL SHOCK. ENTER
> PLATOON SERGEANT)

SERGE   Loyal North Lancs Regiment! Firing squad. Private Jack White.

WHITE   Serves the bastard right. Malingerers like him, skiving off for a bit of frog skirt while we get our bollocks blown away

SERGE   Private Harry Stevens.

STEVE   Forgive me, Hunter.

SERGE   Private Len Smiley.

SMILEY   (WITH DIFFICULTY). N-n-nothing......,

SERGE   Firing Squad - Formation!(COME TO FORMATION)

WHITE   Times like this, some of them can't even hold the rifle steady. Me? Steady as a rock. Bullet straight to the heart

SERGE   Firing Squad - One step forward! (DO SO)

STEVE   Forgive me

SERGE   Firing Squad - Present arms! (DO SO)

SMILEY   Private...Private.... Loyal North........North......

SERGE	Firing squad – take aim (DO SO)
WHITE	He had his fun. And he left the rest of us in the shit
SERGE	Firing Squad - (SERGE RAISES HIS ARM WITH A HANKY IN IT. SLOWLY BRINGS IT DOWN. THERE IS A LOUD EXPLOSION OF GUNFIRE MORPHING INTO THE GENERAL SOUNDS OF WAR, LIGHTING EFFECT. EXIT ALL. WAR SOUNDS RECEDE. HUNTER STEPS FORWARD AND WHILE SPEAKING PREPARES HIMSELF FOR SCENE TWO, SINGING OR LISTENING TO A SONG OF THE TIME AS HE DOES SO – 'OH WE DON'T WANT TO LOSE YOU.')

SCENE TWO

(HUNTER ALREADY ON STAGE IN CIVVY CLOTHES. ENTER BELLA)

BELLA	Have you been avoiding me, Billy Hunter?
HUNTER	Course not, Bella
BELLA	I've been looking all over Shields for you
HUNTER	I've been busy, man
BELLA	You know what me mam says?
HUNTER	I don't know what your man says, no
BELLA	Me mam says you're feckless. What's feckless mean?
HUNTER	Haven't a clue
BELLA	Anyway, that's what you are, according to me mam. Feckless. Sometimes I get frightened
HUNTER	Frightened?

BELLA	This war and everything. You could be signing up soon
HUNTER	Me? I'm not getting blown to bits. Other buggers can do that
BELLA	You do want us to get engaged sometime Billy, don't you?
HUNTER	Why aye, man
BELLA	I mean, you are serious about me?
HUNTER	Look at me
BELLA	I am looking
HUNTER	There you are, then
BELLA	Sometimes I think it's all pretend with you
HUNTER	Do you?
BELLA	Me mam thinks I'm wasting my time
HUNTER	Me and you's got bugger all to do with your mam
BELLA	I just need to know – well, that it's real
HUNTER	Give us a cuddle, Bella (THEY CUDDLE))
BELLA	You never seem to want to talk about things
HUNTER	What things?
BELLA	Just – things. It makes you feel close, talking about things

HUNTER   You get fed up with people talking, man. People telling you what you should do, what you should think. Women waving banners in the streets, them bloody Irish -

BELLA   I'm not trying to tell you what to do

HUNTER   You sure?

BELLA   Course not. It doesn't mean we can't talk

HUNTER   We're talking now

BELLA   We do have a future don't we, Billy Hunter?

HUNTER   A future?

BELLA   When this war's over. I mean, You do think about the future, don't you?

HUNTER   I suppose I must do, aye

BELLA   Because some time I want us to get married and have some lovely babies. That is what you want as well, isn't it, Billy?

HUNTER   Well, aye, I mean..........

BELLA   Making something real Billy. Just me and you

HUNTER   Aye

BELLA   I think I'll go now, Billy

HUNTER   Alright, pet

BELLA   I do love you, Billy

HUNTER   Aye, I reckon you do and all

BELLA   What about me?

HUNTER   What about you?

BELLA   What about you, loving me?

HUNTER   I told you I did, didn't I? The other month

BELLA   I suppose so

HUNTER   (HE CUDDLES HER). You worry too much, Bella

BELLA   And you don't seem to worry at all (EXITS. ENTER
               ARMY RECRUITING OFFICER, SERGEANT & LAD,
               TAYLOR)

RO   This way son. You'll be in the British Army before
               you can say Jack Robinson

LAD   Can't wait, sir!

RO   Ron Taylor will make a fine soldier, wouldn't you say,
               Sergeant?

SERGE   First class material, sir

LAD   You think so sergeant?

SERGE   Absolutely first class, son!

LAD   First class hey? Hear that Billy Hunter – Taylor's first
               first class! (OTHERS CLOCK HUNTER. APPROACH
               HIM)

HUNTER   Not what his lass says.......

RO   You look a big strong Shields lad. Clever lad,
               wouldn't you say, Sergeant?

SERGE   I'd say that, yes, sir

RO	The kind of lad who should be helping his country defeat a savage and cruel enemy
SERGE	And be proud to do so, sir!
RO	How old are you son?
HUNTER	What?
RO	Old enough to serve your nation I would say. What's your name lad?
HUNTER	Tarzan of the Apes (SERGE GRABS HIM)
SERGE	A bit of politeness when addressing the officer, lad
RO	Why do you reckon this big strong Shields lad isn't queuing up to volunteer for the British army, sergeant?
SERGE	All I can think of sir, is that he's happy to live in the finest country in the world, but is not prepared to defend the benefits and freedoms that country brings when threatened by a pitiless and savage foe
RO	I'd call that selfishness, wouldn't you sergeant?
SERGE	I would sir, yes
RO	Perhaps it doesn't worry this lad that we might be overrun by a race of heathens reputed to eat their own children
SERGE	I've heard those Germans would disembowel you, as soon as look at you, sir
HUNTER	You're crackers, you two
RO	Now listen, lad. We're not particularly fond of malingerers here

SERGE	Those who expect others to do their dirty work for them
RO	Where would we be if we all took the same attitude as you?
HUNTER	I don't give a toss for any of that
SERGE	I've told you before son, a bit of politeness in front of an officer. You should take this lad Taylor as an example
HUNTER	Taylor?
SERGE	Proud to serve King and Country., aren't you lad?
LAD	Course I am, yes sir! It's the British. Expeditionary Force for me!
HUNTER	Good for him
SERGE	Proud to wear the uniform of the British Army, eh?
LAD	Yes sir! And to get a real live gun!
HUNTER	Don't shoot yourself in the foot, will you?
RO	So you know this joker, do you?
LAD	Everyone knows Billy Hunter. He fillets fish here on the quay
RO	This Hunter fellow should ingest a little of that your own patriotic fervour
LAD	Ye what?
SERGE	He should enlist
LAD	I can't see that, like

RO   And why not? Something wrong with the Hunter lad is there? Well?

LAD   Billy Hunter's only interested in Billy Hunter. And he thinks with his dick. You ask my lass. Tried it on with her, he did

RO   I see. At ease lad. Did you catch that, sergeant?

SERGE   I got the gist of it, yes sir!

RO   Possibly we'll keep a close eye on Mr.William Hunter in the near future Sergeant. Meantime maybe we should give his 'dick' something to think about

SERGE   Exactly right, sir! (KICKS HUNTER IN THE GROIN. HUNTER DOUBLES UP)

RO   Stand at ease, future Private William Hunter. We've got your number now

SERGE   And don't you forget it, lad

RO   Sergeant. Son (EXIT R.O., SERGE AND LAD)

HUNTER Bastards! (ENTER MARGARET, HIS MOTHER)

MARG   Billy, what's the matter?

HUNTER Nowt, mam

MARG   Have you been hurt, Billy?

HUNTER Nah. Bit of gut ache. Must have been them pickled herrings off the fish quay

MARG   You sure you're alright?

HUNTER Yeah, yeah.

MARG   You weren't home for your tea

HUNTER   Looking for some work, wasn't I? Them trawlermen
                on strike, hardly a fish being landed at the quay

MARG   And did you find any work?

HUNTER   There's bugger all in Shields, man. Not for the likes
                of me

MARG   Have you seen Bella?

HUNTER   Bella, aye

MARG   You shouldn't treat Bella like you do, Billy

HUNTER   Don't know what you're talking about, mam

MARG   She's a decent lass, and a kind one. And she loves you

HUNTER   I suppose she does, aye

MARG   So treat her right

HUNTER   Aye, I will (SHIP'S HOOTER SOUNDS. HUNTER
                PAUSES TO LISTEN)

MARG   Your father's putting flags up outside the house

HUNTER   Aye, I've seen them

MARG   Your father's proud of this country. He says Mr.
                Asquith knows what to do about Germany

HUNTER   That's right

MARG   The country's crazy for war, Billy. Flags, drums,
                posters, everywhere. They're even recruiting out on
                the street

HUNTER   I've heard that, aye

MARG   They're just crazy for it

HUNTER   They're crazy, alright

MARG   Your father says everyone's got to do their bit. Even those troublesome Irish

HUNTER   And what do you say, mam?

MARG   I don't know what to say

HUNTER   Up for the war, are you?

MARG   If your dad says it's alright – (HOOTER SOUNDS AGAIN. BILLY CLOCKS IT)

HUNTER   Listen mam, I might need to go off for a bit

MARG   Off? What do you mean?

HUNTER   Sod all here for me. I might need to get away from all – this

MARG   All what?

HUNTER   Just – well, I might need to get away for a while, that's all

MARG   Joining up, you mean?

HUNTER   Nah – I don't mean that. (HOOTER AGAIN) Hear that, mam?

MARG   There's lots of big boats coming into the Tyne right now

HUNTER   And leaving it... Imagine being on one of them boats. Looking back and seeing all this lot disappear over the horizon

MARG   Join the Royal Navy, you mean?

HUNTER   Nah. A merchant boat, Just sod off somewhere

MARG   You're thinking of – just going.

HUNTER   Why not?

MARG   But your family. And Bella. And friends and –

HUNTER   What about them?

MARG   Just like that?

HUNTER   Yeah. I've had enough of here

MARG   Oh Billy. You'll break your mother's heart one day, I know you will (BILLY DONS HIS MERCHANT NAVY GEAR, SLINGS HIS BAG OVER HIS SHOULDER, AND BOARDS A SHIP, MAYBE A WHEEL-ON GANGPLANK IS BROUGHT ON. TAKES ONE LAST LOOK AT NORTH SHIELDS. WHEELED OFF. GANGPLANK WHEELED BACK ON FOR DISEMBARKATION IN MONTREAL ALONG WITH OTHER SAILORS).

SCENE THREE

(DISEMBARK. SCENE IS A ROWDY BAR IN MONTREAL. AT ONE TABLE ARE SAT JULIETTE, HER HUSBAND AND PARTY, OBVIOUSLY A BIT DRUNK. ENTER BILLY AND HIS MERCHANT NAVY MATE JOE. BILLY AND JULIETTE CLOCK EACH OTHER STRAIGHT AWAY. BILLY AND JOE SIT AT THE NEXT TABLE. JULIETTE GETS UP TO GO TO BAR, PASSES THE OTHER TABLE. BILLY STOPS HER)

HUNTER   Canny dress, pet

JULIETTE   You're an English boy?

HUNTER   Aye, Geordie lad

JULIETTE   First time in Montreal, yes?

HUNTER   That's right pet. Is that your husband?

JULIETTE   The fat pig, yes

HUNTER   Not like me, eh?

JULIETTE   You are a thin pig

HUNTER   I'm not a pig at all

JULIETTE   All men are pigs

HUNTER   He looks pretty drunk

JULIETTE   He is like a barrel of cognac (SHE GOES TO BAR
            FOR DRINK, WHEN SHE RETURNS, BILLY STOPS
            HER AGAIN)

HUNTER   Are all the Montreal women like you, then?

JULIETTE   Like me?

HUNTER   Aye, fantastic. The fat pig looks like he's going to pass
            out any minute

JULIETTE   Then he will grunt and snore for three hours

HUNTER   A lot can happen in three hours

JULIETTE   I afraid of him. He is a bad man

HUNTER   I'm a bit of a bad boy meself

JULIETTE   And I am an unhappy woman

HUNTER   Course you are pet. You could show me the sights

JULIETTE   The sights?

HUNTER   Aye, the sights of Montreal. We've got three hours. You said so. Bet you've got some sights to show yourself, eh?

JULIETTE   You talk naughty. The fat pig would kill me. He would kill you

HUNTER   He's pissed as a rat, man. He's nodding off now. look. He'll not kill no-one

JULIETTE   What you want with me?

HUNTER   What do you think?

JULIETTE   You want to love me?

HUNTER   That's right, aye

JULIETTE   You play with me

HUNTER   Listen pet, you can sit and watch the fat pig snore for three hours or you can come with me. Dead simple

JULIETTE   A woman needs love

HUNTER   I'm your man. Tell them you had to go home. Headache or something, a woman's thing. I'll wait for you outside (SHE HESITATES) Go on then (SHE GOES. BILLY TURN TO SAILOR JOE) I've scored man

JOE   Are you screwing her?

HUNTER   Easy as falling off a log

JOE You should watch out Billy. Her husband's a right nasty piece of work

HUNTER Serves him right then.

JOE It'll drop off one of these days.

HUNTER See you back at the boat (JULIETTE AND HUNTER EXIT BAR).

SCENE FOUR
(DOCKSIDE. BILLY AND JULIETTE ENTER. THEY HAVE JUST FINISHED)

JULIETTE Say you love me, English boy

HUNTER Aye, that's right pet. Things to do though

JULIETTE Do not send me back to fat pig

HUNTER I'm not sending you anywhere. But I've got to go

JULIETTE You play with me

HUNTER I like playing. Nice though, eh?

JULIETTE Please, I –

HUNTER You'll be alright, pet. Thanks. It was bloody good, I'll tell you that.

JULIETTE So what is your name, English boy?

(JOE RUNS UP TO HUNTER)

JOE Hunter! There's two gorillas waiting for you

HUNTER Waiting for me? Says who?

JOE	Says that fat guy whose wife you've just been screwing up some alley. (JULIETTE EXITS QUICKLY) They're out to kill you
HUNTER	Kill me?
JOE	You messed with the wrong bloke Billy. He's a big man in this town. I've seen how he works.
HUNTER	I'll get on the boat man —we don't sail for a few hours. They'll get bored and sod off.
JOE	I tell you, those guys will wait there till the boat's sailed. They're serious
HUNTER	Is there another gangplank?
JOE	That's the only one
HUNTER	So let's sort 'em out, Joe, me and you
JOE	They're armed. I've seen the knives. Guns too, I wouldn't wonder. You're in the shit, Billy
HUNTER	Yeah? Well I've been in the shit before
JOE	So how you going to get out of this one?
HUNTER	I'm thinking (BEAT), Them other English sailors we saw tonight - what was their boat called?
JOE	The Crystal.
HUNTER	That'll do me
JOE	You mean –
HUNTER	I want you to nip onboard here Joe, get my kit out of the cabin. I'll be waiting for you round the corner

JOE   You jumping ship?

HUNTER   You got any better ideas?

JOE   The Crystal docks in Liverpool – the wrong side of
               England for you

BILLY   Yeah, well maybe Shields is the wrong side of
               England for me now. Always fancied a trip to
               Merseyside

JOE   All this trouble for a bit of skirt. Is it worth it?

HUNTER   It's always worth it. Just get the gear, OK?

JOE   Alright, I will. But you need to sort yourself out,
               Billy Hunter

HUNTER   Thanks for the lecture Joe. I'd better get lost (EXIT)

JOE   Yeah, right. (MIMICS)'Oh, and thanks for doing
               all this for me as well Joe' – 'Oh, don't mention it,
               Billy...' 'Well, no I won't'
               (EXIT JOE)

SCENE FIVE

               (WHITE, STEVENS AND SMILEY ARE IN THE
               BAR, HUNTER IS WATCHING)

WHITE   You're on, Smiley.

STEVENS   Three... Two... One... go!

               (THEY ARM WRESTLE, WHITE WINS)

WHITE   You owe me another beer.

HUNTER   Eh, Scouser, want another go?

WHITE   Don't swear at me, I'm not a Scouser, I'm from
                  Manchester.

                  (WHITE AND HUNTER ARM WRESTLE,
                  HUNTER WINS)

HUNTER   Like I said, a Scouser is no match for a Geordie

WHITE   Maybe you're tougher than you look. So what's a
                  Geordie git doing in Liverpool anyway?

HUNTER   Just signed off the boat

WHITE   And now what?

HUNTER   Who knows? I'm a free man

STEVENS   None of us is free, Geordie

HUNTER   Well, I am

SMILEY   Why not come with us, me and White and Stevens?

HUNTER   With you?

SMILEY   We're all signing up. You could arm wrestle with
                  Fritz then! Look out Kaiser Bill! Here we come!

HUNTER   Don't fancy getting me John Thomas shot off in
                  France, thanks

WHITE   Coward, eh?

SMILEY   Maybe he's got a posh job in a posh office lined up.
                  Or maybe he's got a nice little woman waiting for him
                  somewhere

WHITE   Or maybe he is a coward. Afraid of loud bangs. Afraid
                  of Germans

HUNTER   I'm afraid of nowt

SMILEY   I can't wait. Just six week's training, then all that lovely warm sun. All them sexy Senoritas!

STEVENS   That's Spain, Smiley. It's Madamoiselles in France

SMILEY   Well, you know... I fancy some of that vin rug as well

STEVENS   You mean vin rouge

SMILEY   Yeah well, that wine stuff. Oooh lah lah!

WHITE   I can't wait to kill some Germans

SMILEY   Anyhow, it'll be a laugh – it'll be like a paid holiday!

HUNTER   Is that why you're joining up Stevens– for a holiday?

STEVENS   No

HUNTER   Why then?

STEVENS   Good question

HUNTER   You're a funny set of mates

STEVENS   Who said we're mates?

SMILEY   We're joining the Loyal North Lancs regiment. Left right, left right, left right!

HUNTER   Aye, good luck and all. Do *you* fancy an arm-wrestle?

STEVENS   I'd be no contest

WHITE   Are you chicken?

HUNTER   Give it a crack, man!

STEVENS   Alright (THEY PREPARE)

HUNTER   So when do you do it – this volunteering lark?

STEVENS   Not long now

SMILEY   I've never been abroad. Except to the Isle of Man
            once – I was seasick waiting for the ferry!

STEVENS   He thinks it'll be a bit of fun, this war

HUNTER   What about him? (INDICATING WHITE)

STEVENS   White? He can taste the war on his lips

HUNTER   And you?

STEVENS   Let's wrestle (THEY GET READY)

SMILEY   Oooh – look at this! Scouse versus Geordie, part two

WHITE   Don't cheat this time, Geordie lad

HUNTER   Cheat?

WHITE   You know what I mean

HUNTER   I beat you fair and square, man

WHITE   Oh yeah?

SMILEY   After three. One – two – three (THEY ARM
            WRESTLE. FAIRLY EVEN. ENTER ANGELA. SHE
            IS OBVIOUSLY A DISTRACTION FOR HUNTER)

HUNTER   Who the bloody hell – (HIS STRENGTH BEGINS TO
            FADE AWAY)

SMILEY   That's Angela!

WHITE   She's a sexy bleeder

STEVENS   You like Angela eh, Hunter?

SMILEY   Everyone likes Angela. And Angela likes us. Because we're signing up. (HUNTER ABANDONS THE ARM WRESTLING)

HUNTER   Have you had her?

STEVENS   Not yet

WHITE   We will though. All three of us!

SMILEY   Just as soon as we sign up on that dotted line!

HUNTER   How do you mean?

STEVENS   You might say Angela's what brings us three together

SMILEY   Come together, eh!

HUNTER   You mean she'll screw anyone who signs up?

WHITE   Not anyone

SMILEY   Just us!

WHITE   How come you're keeping us waiting, anyway Angela? You know you want it

SMILEY   Steady White! You have to handle Angela with care!

HUNTER   Who is she then, this - Angela?

STEVENS   A force of nature. A blinding flash of beauty in a dark world

WHITE   He talks shite. She's a shag waiting to happen

STEVENS   Cut it out, White

WHITE   Oh, we're offending the poet

HUNTER   Poet?

WHITE   Aye. Didn't you know? He's quite a little
              Wordsworth, is Stevens. Wait till the Germans hear
              we've got a poet with us. They'll probably surrender
              straight up

SMILEY   I dreamt of Angela last night. Honest! (HUNTER
              TAKES THE OPPORTUNITY TO GO TO ANGELA)

WHITE   You? The bloody virgin?

SMILEY   I'm not a virgin - I - –

WHITE   You couldn't get it up if you tried

SMILEY   Course I could – I

STEVENS   She likes Hunter

WHITE   No accounting for taste

STEVENS   She likes him a lot. I think she likes you more than
              any of us

SMILEY   She wants him to be one of us, don't you see? We
              could be together, all four of us! A real adventure.
              Like in the comics! Real soldiers!

STEVENS   Maybe you could teach Hunter to be a man, White.
              Out there in the heat of battle. What do you think?

WHITE   I could teach the Geordie that, alright

SMILEY   Angela could teach him to be a man as well!

SMILEY   The adventure starts here eh? Us four! We
            were all meant to meet up, can't you see? The
            adventure starts here (HUNTER GOES INTO
            LONG PASSIONATE EMBRACE WITH ANGELA.
            RECRUITING OFFICER STANDS)

RO   Volunteer number one! (WHITE COMES
            FORWARD) Attention! Name, address, age! Sign
            there! (DOES SO) At ease! The King's Shilling!
            (HANDS OVER)Volunteer number two!
            (WHITE MOVES OFF. SMILEY ENTERS)
            Attention! Name, address, age! Sign there! (SIGNS)
            At ease! The King's Shilling! Volunteer number
            three! (SMILEY MOVES OFF. STEVENS COMES
            FORWARD) Attention! Name, address, age. Sign
            there! (SIGNS) At ease! The Kings's Shilling Recruit
            number four! (STEVENS MOVES OFF. HUNTER
            HESITATES) Recruit number four! (ANGELA
            KISSES HIM AGAIN AND ENCOURAGES HIM.
            HUNTER EVENTUALLY COMES FORWARD)
            Attention! Name, address, age! Sign there!
            (HESITATION) I said lad, sign there! (SIGNS) At
            ease! The King's Shilling!(THE NEW RECRUITS GO
            THROUGH TRAINING, ENDING UP AT WESTERN
            FRONT)

SCENE SIX

            (A FEW MILES BEHIND THE WESTERN FRONT.
            ENTER SERGEANT)

SERGE   Attention! (THEY COME TO ATTENTION.
            SERGEANT WALKS ALONG THEM INSPECTING
            THEM). I'm your Platoon Sergeant, No. 3 Platoon.
            Well, I've seen some sights in my life, but you lot take
            the biscuit. (YELLS INTO SOLDIER NO.1'S EAR)
            What is it you lot take, lad?

SOLD 1   The biscuit, sergeant!

SERGE	The biscuit, that's right. Now then, they tell me you lot should be ready for battle. Properly trained they tell me. You could have fooled me. Let's find out what pathetic cast-offs from humanity we have amongst us, shall we? (TO STEVENS) Name!
STEVE	Private Stevens, sergeant
SERGE	You look a bit pasty to me, Stevens. Can't have British soldiers looking pasty now, can we?
STEVE	No sergeant
SERGE	No sergeant. Fritz would think we were going soft. A bit of time in the trenches will put some colour in your cheeks, Stevens. Nothing like the feel of cold mud round your knackers to concentrate the mind. You got the makings of a soldier Stevens?
STEVE	Not sure, sergeant
SERGE	Not sure, sergeant.......(SHOUTS) Well you bloody well better be sure lad, and quick about it, or you'll be dead before you have time to scratch your arse. Got that?
STEVE	Yes sergeant
SERGE	I didn't hear you, lad!
STEVE	(SHOUTS) Yes, Sergeant!
WHITE	He writes poetry, Sergeant
SERGE	What?
WHITE	That one. He writes poetry
SERGE	Is that right, Private Stevens. You write poetry?

STEVE   Yes sergeant

SERGE   Yes, well. I've heard about some of you bloody poets.
                  So watch it. Right. What's your name, lad?

SMILEY   Private Smiley, sergeant!

SERGE   Smiley, eh? Well this place should give you
                  something to smile about. It's a laugh a minute here
                  and no mistake! Ever had a German bayonet up your
                  arse, Smiley?

SMILEY   Can't say I have sergeant, no

SERGE   Try and keep it that way, lad. Did I see you looking
                  almost cheerful there?

SMILEY   I do like to keep cheerful wherever possible,
                  sergeant!

SERGE   Wherever possible, eh Smiley? (SHOUTS) Well,
                  it's not possible here! You're in a war lad, a messy,
                  bloody, painful, stinking, foul fuck-up of a war. You'll
                  be crawling with lice soon enough, You might get
                  pneumonia in a few days. And within a very short
                  time you'll wish you'd never been born, that's if
                  you're still alive of course, which is very debatable,
                  cos the chances are you'll be burnt alive by a flame-
                  thrower, choked to death by poisonous gas, blown
                  into a million pieces by a whiz-bang, cut in two by a
                  machine gun, or drowned in a flooded shell hole .
                  Got that have you?

SMILEY   I think I have, Sergeant

SERGE   You think you have?

SMILEY   That is, I know I have, Sergeant

SERGE	So we'll hear no more cheery rubbish from you, Smiley!
SMILEY	Yes, sergeant. I mean no, sergeant
SERGE	(TO SOLDIER NO. 2) Missing your mummy, lad?
SOLD. 2	Oh yes, sergeant!
SERGE	Yes, sergeant? What kind of sentimental soft as shite poncy weakling says something like that.
SOLD. 2	I just thought –
SERGE	This war is no place for mummys' boys, lad! Got that?
SOLD. 3	Yes, sergeant
SERGE	Yes sergeant. You do not miss your mummy. That's an order. Well?
SOLD. 2	I do not miss my mummy, Sergeant!
SERGE	(MOVES ON) Name!
WHITE	Private White, sergeant!
SERGE	And what's bugging you, Private White?
WHITE	I can't wait to kill some Germans, Sergeant!
SERGE	Don't like Germans eh, White?
WHITE	I don't like them one little bit, Sergeant!
SERGE	That's what I like to hear
WHITE	The only useful German is a dead German

SERGE   You like being in the British Army, Private White?

WHITE   I like it very much, Sergeant.

SERGE   The army's my life. I live for the army Private White. Understand that can you?

WHITE   I can understand that perfectly, yes, Sergeant.

SERGE   Only two things important in this life. The army and family. Got that?

WHITE   That could have been me talking there, Serge.

SERGE   Carry on Private White. (TO SOLDIER NO.3) You lad. Missing your mummy?

SOLD. 3   No Sergeant!

SERGE   Not missing your mummy? What kind of insensitive uncaring bastard doesn't miss his mummy out here!

SOLD. 3   But I thought you said –

SERGE   Never mind what I said, lad

SOLD. 3   Sorry sergeant!

SERGE   You will be lad, you will be. You miss your mummy. And that's an order! Well?

SOLD. 2   But what about me, Sergeant, I don't understand, I –

SERGE   I said he does miss his mummy. That means it must be true because I've said it. If I say a wet fart sounds like a symphony orchestra then that's what a wet fart sounds like. Is that crystal clear?

SOLD. 2   Yes, sergeant!

SERGE	So what does a wet fart sound like?
SOLD. 2	Sorry, Sergeant?
SERGE	A wet fart – what does it sound like
SOLD. 2	It sounds like – like what you said
SERGE	Any idea what a symphony orchestra sounds like, lad?
SOLD. 2	No, sergeant!
SERGE	Ever listened to a symphony?
SOLD. 2	Can't say I have, no sergeant
SERGE	Me neither. But you'd know a wet fart if you heard one?
SOLD. 2	Yes, sergeant
SERGE	So soldier, are you missing your mummy?
SOLD. 3	I am missing my mummy, yes sergeant!
SERGE	Good (PASSES ON TO HUNTER) And what kind of specimen do we have here? Name!
HUNTER	Private Hunter, sergeant
SERGE	Hunter – good name for a soldier. Do you hate Germans, Hunter?
HUNTER	Never met one, sergeant!
SERGE	Did I ask you if you'd ever met one, Hunter? I asked, did you hate them? Well?
HUNTER	Whatever you say, sergeant!

SERGE   Not whatever I say lad, whatever you say. Do you hate Germans?

HUNT   I'd prefer a nice blonde, sergeant

SERGE   I could slap you on a charge, Hunter. Insubordination, disrespect for a superior. You're a bloody toe-rag, aren't you?

HUNT   Who knows, sergeant?

SERGE   A bloody Geordie toe rag as well. The worst kind. Did you know you were an inferior human being, Hunter?

HUNT   Can't say I ever knew that, sergeant, no

SERGE   Because I am your superior Hunter, and that makes you an inferior being. (TO ALL) That's right, isn't it? (NO RESPONSE) I said that's right, isn't it?

ALL   Yes, sergeant!

SERGE   None of you make any mistake about that? Alright? (SOLDIERS MURMUR) I said, alright?

ALL   Yes, sergeant

SERGE   (CONFIDES TO HUNTER) You'll not get the better of me, Hunter. I've got your card marked. Got it?

HUNT   Card, sergeant?

SERGE   Well and truly marked. One inch out of line, and you're a gonner

HUNT   (OUT LOUD) Thank you very much, Sergeant! Much appreciated, Sergeant!

SERGE	I eat cheeky bastards like you for dinner (TO ALL) Now then. You think I'm a monster. You think I'm an unfeeling cruel beast. And you'll all come to hate me just as much as you hate the stinking freezing mud hole you'll soon be stuck in. We'll all be on the front line soon, where our job is to sit around and freeze to death till the order comes to go over the top. You can expect a gas attack any time. Rule number one – always keep your gas mask close to your person. Right, we march at 4pm. Any questions? Good. I don't like questions. Get yourselves sorted out (EXITS. DURING REST OF SCENE THEY PREPARE TO MARCH)
HUNTER	He's a bloody nutter
STEVE	No more than anyone else here
HUNTER	He can go screw himself
WHITE	You're heading for big trouble Hunter, you know that?
HUNTER	I can look after myself
SMILEY	That Sergeant frightens me
WHITE	A baby would frighten you
SMILE	It wouldn't!
WHITE	The sergeant's got it all under control. He knows what's what
STEVE	And what exactly is what?
WHITE	This is what's what. (THRUSTS HIS BAYONET INTO STEVENS FACE) Feel it, can you? Through the tunic – through the flesh - through the bone and finally out again through Fritz's back.

WHITE (cont) (TO HUNTER) Alright, Hunter?

HUNTER I'm alright

WHITE Thinking of Angela? Funny where a good screw can land you, isn't it? In the middle of a war

HUNTER What would you know about a good screw, White?

WHITE More than you think, lover boy. And a bit more than him (INDICATES SMILEY) You couldn't get it up with Angela, Smiley, could you?.

SMILEY Course I could!

WHITE As limp as a lettuce I heard -

SMILEY That's ridiculous, I –

STEVE Leave him alone, White

WHITE Curled up like a little pink shrimp

SMILEY Sod off.

WHITE Silly little prick

HUNTER You need teaching a lesson, White

WHITE What, by some Geordie ponce?
(ENTER SERGEANT.)

SERGE All right lads? Good! (WHISTLE SOUNDS). Hear that? Time to move out. Unfix bayonets! (DO SO) Platoon! Ready to march! (GET THEMSELVES ORGANISED).Platoon! By the right – march. Left, right, left right, left, right.....(PLATOON MARCHES OFF, OUR FOUR PLUS SUPPORT. AS THEY MARCH SOUNDS OF BATTLE GROW SLOWLY BUT INCREASINGLY LOUDER.

END MARCH NEAR THE FRONT LINE).
Platoon – fall out! (THEY SETTLE IN. NIGHT
FALLS. THEY SLEEP)

SCENE SEVEN

SERGE	Right settle down lads, big day tomorrow. Can't sleep White?
WHITE	Not really Serg.
SERGE	Thinking about home?
WHITE	Yeah.
SERGE	You'll be alright son.
WHITE	You got a family Serge?

(SERGE TAKES PHOTO FROM HIS POCKET)

SERGE	My wife Dorothy. My kids Tom and Janet
WHITE	Any man would be proud of a family like that, Serge
SERGE	She's the one for me White. Same with her
WHITE	I understand, Serge
SERGE	Wants to follow me in the army, young Tom. Janet – well, who knows?
WHITE	A family's the thing, Serge
SERGE	Yes. Well, that will be all, Private White (SERGE STARTS TO WAKE THE OTHERS UP)
SERGE	This is it lads, this is what you've had all those wet dreams about. We're going over the top (THEY PREPARE)

WHITE	What's it like over there, Serge?
SERGE	It's a doddle. The wire's been cut so you're straight through, and my guess is you'll find hardly a single German behind the lines. They'll all either have been blown to bits from our bombardment, or have buggered off back to Berlin
WHITE	Typical cowardly bastards. I'm ready for this! How about you, Smiley?
SMILEY	Course I am
WHITE	You were crying last night in your sleep?
SMILEY	I wasn't I -,
WHITE	Sobbing like a baby. How about you Hunter?
HUNTER	Sort yourself out White. I'll manage
WHITE	Just trying to be helpful Hunter. Stevens?
STEVE	What?
WHITE	The poet's ready for battle, is he? (NO REPLY)
SERGE	Get yourselves sorted now, lads. Fix bayonets! (THEY DO SO) Walk, don't run. Arms length apart. When in doubt, go forward. Remember? When in doubt, go forward. This is it, you boys. You'll be fine, You'll all be fine (A WAIT. THEN THE WHISTLE. THEY GO OVER THE TOP. DISAPPEAR. BLINDING LIGHT, SOUND OF GUNFIRE AND BATTLE VERY LOUD.)

SCENE EIGHT
(A VISUAL SCENE OF MEN IN BATTLE WITH LIGHTING AND SOUND EFFECTS).

SCENE NINE

(POST BATTLE. PLAINTIVE SOUND OF SOLITARY
TRUMPETER. ENTER SERGEANT WITH HIS
ROLL CALL OF SOLDIERS. STANDS CENTRE
STAGE).

SERGE   Right lads. Answer your name when you hear it.
Allerton!

V/O   Here serge!

SERGE   Andrews!

V/O   Here, serge!

SERGE   Beaumont! (SILENCE) Beaumont! (SILENCE)
Bentley! (SILENCE) Bentley! (SILENCE)

SMILEY   He had no head

WHITE   Ye what?

SMILEY   Blown clean off. And the body. Still moving. A body
with no head. Like –

WHITE   Like what?

SMILEY   Like it didn't matter

WHITE   It don't matter

SMILEY   Then it stopped moving. Lifeless flesh. As lifeless as a
carcass hanging in a butcher's shop

WHITE   And a lot less bloody use (BACK TO ROLL CALL)

SERGE   Dawson!

V/O   Here, serge

SERGE   English

V/O   Here serge!

SERGE   Gregory! (SILENCE) Gregory! (SILENCE) Harris!

V/O   Here, serge!

SERGE   Houghton! (SILENCE) Houghton! (SILENCE)
             Hunter! (SILENCE. SLIGHT REACTION FROM
             SERGE) Hunter!

HUNTER   I'm here

SERGE   I'm here – sergeant, if you don't mind Hunter!

HUNTER   I'm here – sergeant.......

SERGE   Leighton!

VO   Here Sergeant.

HUNTER   Bastard. He said the wire had been cut. It hadn't.
             He said there'd be hardly any resistance. There were
             bloody hundreds of them, machine guns, the lot

WHITE   War's not all clean and tidy and predictable Hunter,
             time you learnt that

SERGE   Smiley!

SMILEY   Here Serge!

SERGE   Stevens!

STEVENS   Here Serge!

SERGE   Taylor! (SILENCE) Taylor! (SILENCE. BACK TO
             SOLDIERS)

SERGE   Wallis! (SILENCE) Wallis! (SILENCE) White!

WHITE   Here, Serge! (EXIT WHITE)

SERGE   And finally.....Worthing! (SILENCE) And finally.....
               Worthing! (SILENCE. PAUSE)

HUNT   He doesn't frighten me

STEVE   One enemy's enough out here Hunter. You need to
               be careful

HUNTER   How do you mean?

STEVE   The sergeant, White. Just be careful, that's all

VOICES   Gas! Gas! Gas!

               (CHAOS ENSUES AS THE TRENCH IS ATTACKED
               BY GAS. WHITE CAN'T FIND HIS MASK AND
               THE SERGE DRAGS HIM OFF BEFORE HE IS
               OVERCOME)

SCENE TEN
               (STEVENS AND HUNTER IN THE TRENCHES.
               HUNTER IS PICKING AT HIS LICE, THEN
               SQUEEZING EACH ONE TO DEATH. SMILEY IS
               HUNCHED IN A CORNER IN A STATE)

STEVE   That gas attack would have killed a lesser man

HUNTER   He's hard as nails, White

STEVE   Know what he just said? No bastard German's going
               to kill me. The doctor can't believe he's recovering at
               all It wasn't you, was it?

HUNTER   What wasn't me?

HUNTER   Hid White's gas mask

HUNTER   Talk sense, man

STEVE   (NOTICES WHAT HUNTER'S DOING) Got lice?

HUNTER   Millions of the little bleeders

STEVE   Killing them like that takes forever

HUNTER   You got a better suggestion?

STEVE   This way, look (LIGHTS CANDLE, PUTS IT UNDER
             TIN LID. PICKS LICE OFF HIS OWN BODY THEN
             THROWS THEM ONTO THE LID WHERE THEY
             SIZZLE AND DIE)

HUNTER   That's neat. Thanks, Stevens

STEVE   You no sooner kill them than there's a
             thousand more

HUNTER   Aye

STEVE   Remind you of anything

HUNTER   How do you mean?

STEVE   These lice. Thrown to the slaughter. But plenty more
             queuing up where they came from

HUNTER   Oh aye

STEVE   (THROWS MORE) There you go. Pop and die. Pop
             and die. A truly noble death as Rupert Brooke might
             have said

HUNTER   Who?

STEVE   Never mind.

HUNTER   Why did you sign up? Me, I just wanted a screw.

STEVE   Half of history is down to people just wanting a screw

HUNTER   Angela the Angel

STEVE   The Angel of Death.

HUNTER   But you didn't sign up just for her, did you?

STEVE   No. But she was part of it. Poets have to see

HUNTER   See what?

STEVE   All this

HUNTER   So now you've seen, have you?

STEVE   I'm seeing all the time

HUNTER   Seeing what?

STEVE   Everything

HUNTER   I think Smiley's cracking up

STEVE   He thought it would all be a big adventure, a laugh.

HUNTER   And White just wanted to kill Germans

STEVE   That kind of simple belief – it's a bit frightening

HUNTER   What you got there?

STEVE   It's part of me seeing, you might say

HUNTER   How do you mean?

STEVE   It's a poem, my bonny Geordie lad

HUNTER   About the war?

STEVE   I think so. I let other people decide what my poems
               are about

HUNTER   You say some bloody weird things. Can I have a look?

STEVE   It's not finished yet.

HUNTER   Later then, soon as you finish it

STEVE   Do you really want to look?

HUNTER   Why not? I've never read much poetry

STEVE   You and the rest of the population (LOUD CRIES
               HEARD IN THE DISTANCE). Listen to them.
               Those poor bastards

SMILEY   Why can't they just shut up and die? Lying out there
               in no man's land like that? Moaning, whimpering,
               hour after hour. I'll shut them up! (MAKES TO GO
               OUT. STEVENS RESTRAINS HIM)

STEVE   Take it easy Smiley. One foot out there and you're at
               the end of a sniper's bullet

SMILEY   Moaning and whimpering. Whimpering and
               moaning......

STEVE   Dying in a muddy field, just one hundred yards
               away. Welcome to the 20th century. We'll all hear
               that sound for the rest of our lives. I need to ask you
               something ,Smiley

SMILEY   What?

STEVENS   White's missing gas mask. Was that anything to do
               with you?

SMILEY   What gas mask?

STEVENS   He could have been dead, you realise that? A long
           slow lingering death from gas, the lungs eaten away
           from the inside

SMILEY   I want to be home. Everton. Mam at the dolly tub.
           Me licking out the cake bowl

STEVENS   Did you hide his gas mask?

SMILEY   Our budgie's called Joey (MORE NOISES OF THE
           DYING) Turn that noise off! Turn it off!
           (ENTER WHITE)

WHITE   You alright Smiley?

STEVENS   It's nothing. No after-effects of the gas, White?

WHITE   It'd take more than a whiff of sodding Jerry gas.
           Some bastard hid my mask

STEVENS   You mislaid it, that's all

WHITE   I've got my own ideas who that bastard was. Eh,
           Hunter?

HUNTER   What?

WHITE   My gas mask – ring any bells?

HUNTER   No bells out here, White

WHITE   I'll sort you out soon enough

HUNTER   Sort yourself out

WHITE   (TO STEVENS) Still writing them stupid poems,
           Stevens

STEVE   Got it in one, White (BUSIES HIMSELF WITH
           WRITING POEM FOR REST OF SCENE)

WHITE   Bloody poets (TO HUNTER) What are you looking so
                   twitchy about?

HUNTER   Twitchy?

WHITE   Yeah, twitchy, you're like a cat on heat

HUNTER   Maybe I am

WHITE   So what's it all about Hunter

HUNTER   You wouldn't understand, White

WHITE   Try me

HUNTER   A man like me – he needs a woman

WHITE   A man like you would shag a dog if it smiled nicely

HUNTER   I've heard some of the women in the village are
                   up for it

WHITE   You'd be lucky

HUNTER   I'm always lucky, White

WHITE   You going to the village then?

HUNTER   I might just do that

WHITE   I'll go with you. Women like me

HUNTER   You?

WHITE   A little runt like you. You'd be lost on your own

HUNTER   Don't think so, White

WHITE   I know what's what, Hunter

HUNTER	Yeah. Well, thanks anyway
WHITE	Better off in twos, Hunter. Better chance of a shag
HUNTER	Not me, mate. I travel light
WHITE	I said, I'll come with you, alright?
HUNTER	And I said, I don't want a big ugly bastard like you around. Alright? Stay here and play with yourself
WHITE	You're asking for it
HUNTER	Not off you though. OK?
SMILEY	(REFERRING TO INJURED) Moaning and whimpering. Moaning and whimpering.......
WHITE	Why don't you shut up Smiley, you bloody runt?
SMILEY	Moan and whimper.......
STEVENS	Finished
HUNTER	The poem? Let's have a look then
WHITE	Don't say the Geordie can read as well?
STEVENS	You want to see the poem?
HUNTER	Why not?
STEVENS	You really want to see it?
HUNTER	Yeah (STEVENS HANDS IT OVER)
WHITE	Maybe you could read it out
HUNTER	Read it out?

WHITE   And I'm sure Stevens would appreciate it

STEVENS   Good to hear someone else read it

WHITE   Go on I could do with a laugh! He'll not read it out!

STEVENS   I think he will

WHITE   And I tell you, he'll not

HUNTER   I bloody will. We're not all pig-ignorant, White.
             (HUNTER PREPARES TO READ OUT POEM)

WHITE   Wait, what's it called?

STEVENS   All warmth is fleeing.

HUNTER   (READS POEM)
             Now he cannot laugh, or cry.
             He feels nothing. He thinks nothing.
             In his top pocket, the photo
             Of his wife and child is unharmed.
             Despite the burst of fire, both survived.

             He will lie for several hours
             In mud which sucks him down.
             A colleague lies close by
             Arm stretched out towards him.
             Still the shells explode
             Bringing cascades of mud and soil
             A falling of earth to earth
             Which gradually and without ceremony
             Will bury him.
             Nothing of him will be seen again.

And still the photo survives
Sealed tight in its small wallet
Sealed tight in the button-down pocket
Of the khaki tunic
Covering a heart, now silent
From which all warmth is fleeing.
(SOUNDS OF DYING MEN IN NO
MAN'S LAND. MUSIC)

(INTERVAL)

PART TWO

SCENE ELEVEN
(IN THE VILLAGE. CLAUDETTE IS CHOPPING WOOD. HUNTER WALKS IN AND SEES HER. OBSERVES HER FOR A TIME. SHE SPOTS HIM)

CLAUD   Why you look at me like that, English boy?

HUNTER   Like what?

CLAUD   Like you look at me

HUNTER   Yeah, well.......You're a cracker, you

CLAUD   Cracker?

HUNTER   Aye

CLAUD   Cracker is bang, bang, yes?

HUNTER   Aye, if you like, pet (SHE CARRIES ON CHOPPING FOR A WHILE THEN PAUSES)

CLAUD   Where you from?

HUNTER   I'm a Shields lad, me

CLAUD   Shiel-eds?

HUNTER   North Shields. Near Newcastle upon Tyne

CLAUD   North Shiel-eds....

HUNTER   I could go for you, pet. Me and you, eh?

CLAUD   Me and you?

HUNTER   Yeah – you know

CLAUD   You only old enough to fight, English boy. Not to love
             (RETURNS TO CHOPPING)

HUNTER   You think I'm a boy, do you?

CLAUD   You not yet born

HUNTER   Got a bit of cheek, you. Loads of lasses have gone
             for me

CLAUD   Gone - gone where?

HUNTER   Just - gone

CLAUD   What is your name?

HUNTER   Hunter. William Hunter

CLAUD   You come to my country to do your hunting. Why
             you fight in my country, William Hunter?

HUNTER   Sod knows

CLAUD   Any fool can fire a gun. You are a fool.

HUNTER   You've got a right gob on you, you know that?

CLAUD   Gob?

HUNTER   You're a bit cocky

CLAUD   Cocky?

HUNTER   Never mind. Hey, how about it? You know (TRIES IT
             ON. SHE PUSHES HIM OFF)

CLAUD   You like to play with women, silly boy?

HUNTER   How do you mean?

CLAUD	You cannot play with me, William Hunter
HUNTER	Sod you, then (BEAT. SHE RETURNS TO CHOPPING) So what's your name, then?
CLAUD	My name does not matter
HUNTER	Come on, what's your name?
CLAUD	My name is Claudette
HUNTER	Calling me a boy!
CLAUD	You not yet born. Why they send boys to fight in my country?
HUNTER	Playing hard to get, is that it
CLAUD	Hard to get?
HUNTER	Prick-teaser. I know your sort!
CLAUD	Preek – teaser.......this is kind of bird, yes? (MAKES BIRD NOISE) 'Preek! Preek! Preek!'
HUNTER	You taking the piss? Look, I haven't got very long
CLAUD	No soldier has got very long
HUNTER	You know what I mean
CLAUD	I know what you mean, William Hunter. Go back to your army
HUNTER	What – empty-handed?
CLAUD	And empty-headed
HUNTER	I will then. Think I need you?

CLAUD   Yes, you need me. I am not yet born either. Goodbye, William Hunter (PUTS DOWN AXE. EXITS)

HUNTER   (SHOUTS AFTER HER) What the hell does that mean?

SCENE TWELVE
             (NEXT DAY. ON CAMP. SOLDIER ENTERS WITH MAIL. LETTERS DELIVERED TO SERGEANT. SERGEANT OPENS LETTER. WEDDING RING FALLS OUT, READS IT AND SLUMPS. WHITE ENTERS)

WHITE   Alright Serge?

             (SERGE DROPS RING ON FLOOR)

SERGE   Left me? Walked out, kids and all? Left me? For some randy bastard of a salesman? (HE HOLDS UP WEDDING RING. EVENTUALLY HE THROWS AWAY THE RING AND TRIES TO STEADY HIMSELF. WHITE PICKS UP RING. HANDS IT BACK TO SERGEANT. THEY HEAR OTHERS APPROACHING. LOOK AT ONE ANOTHER)

WHITE   (HANDS LETTERS TO WHITE) Carry on White. (GOES TO EXIT)

STEVENS   Sergeant.

HUNTER   Serge. (SERGE PAUSES)... ant.

STEVENS   Going to the village again?

HUNTER   Aye

STEVENS   Anything special?

HUNTER   Nah. Well – might bump into this lass. Right cheeky sod, mind

STEVENS   You like her?

HUNTER   Like her? She's too bloody cocky

STEVENS   But you're going back to see her

HUNTER   Who said I was going to see her?

STEVENS   Fair enough......

HUNTER   The thing is you see - (ENTER WHITE)

WHITE   Geordie (HANDS LETTER)

HUNTER   Scouse.

WHITE   Stevens... oh no it says Smiley, he's with the M.O
            (GOES TO EXIT)

HUNTER   See you later Stevens.

WHITE   The bloody Geordie's off again.

HUNTER   That a problem, White?

WHITE   I told you. You should let me go with you

HUNTER   And I told you to piss off

WHITE   You'd have more chance of getting your leg over with
            me around

HUNTER   I'll take that chance

WHITE   Maybe you've scored already, have you? Them
            French tarts must need glasses

HUNTER   Why don't you go off and play with your bayonet?

WHITE   You should be careful what you say to me, Hunter

HUNTER   Oh, should I?

WHITE   Yeah, you should

HUNTER   I'm off. See you later, Stephens (EXITS)

STEPHENS   Good luck (STEPHENS AND WHITE STARE AT
            ONE ANOTHER)

SCENE THIRTEEN
            (THE VILLAGE. A LITTLE LATER. ENTER
            HUNTER. SITS WAITING. ENTER CLAUDETTE)

CLAUD   William Hunter from North Shiel-eds comes back

HUNTER   I needed some stuff from the village, that's all

CLAUD   Thank you for coming back

HUNTER   Yeah well. Like I said, I needed some stuff.

CLAUD   Ah, of course......You have girl in North Shiel-eds

HUNTER   What? Well, not really, no, I –

CLAUD   Why you pretend ,William Hunter

HUNTER   Pretend? I don't know what you mean, I –

CLAUD   Boys always pretend

HUNTER   Look, I'm not a boy, I keep telling you

CLAUD   You have girl in North Shiel-eds?

HUNTER   No.

CLAUD   Still,you pretend (BEAT)

HUNT   Look yeah, yes, I sort of did have a girl there, but -

CLAUD   But what?

HUNTER   Well.....look, I'm not much good with words

CLAUD   Try. It is your language

HUNTER   Well - I felt trapped, see? She's a lovely lass
and - hey, how come I'm telling you all this?

CLAUD   You never tell anyone else?

HUNTER   Nah. Blokes don't talk about things like that

CLAUD   Well?

HUNTER   Well, what?

CLAUD   The story is finished, so soon?

HUNTER   Well, no, I –

CLAUD   What do you say in English, I am altogether ears

HUNTER   Aye, summat like that pet

CLAUD   So? I am altogether ears

HUNTER   Well, you see, Bella - that's her name - she wants to
get married and have bairns -

CLAUD   Bairns?

HUNTER   Aye, that's Geordie for kids, like. Anyhow, I suppose
we should, like, but when I think about it all,
I just feel –

CLAUD   What?

HUNTER   Like I'm suffocating, sinking. I had to get away, see?
Get my freedom

CLAUD	Freedom to sleep with other women?
HUNTER	Something like that
CLAUD	That is freedom?
HUNTER	Why not?
CLAUD	Love is its own freedom
HUNTER	That sounds like clever shite
CLAUD	Shite?
HUNTER	Fancy talk. I've loved loads of lasses
CLAUD	You have never loved
HUNTER	Oh yeah? How come you know so much about it?
CLAUD	Only once in life can we love
HUNTER	That's bollocks
CLAUD	Only once. The rest is – Pretty songs, perfume, pretend
HUNTER	You're bloody weird you.
CLAUD	I have never loved either
HUNTER	Ye what?
CLAUD	Like you, I am still not born
HUNTER	You don't talk much like lasses in Shields.
CLAUD	Your army marched through my village
HUNTER	Aye, we did

CLAUD	Many soldiers. All same uniform. Many many soldiers. But I saw only one
HUNTER	Eh?
CLAUD	I saw the boy, Hunter
HUNTER	You fancied me?
CLAUD	I saw the boy who I could make a man. The boy who could make me a woman
HUNTER	Make you a woman?
CLAUD	You understand?
HUNTER	Not sure.
CLAUD	Only once in life can we love. Now. Here. (BEAT).
HUNTER	Yeah? And how long does it last, this love of yours?
CLAUD	How do we know?
HUNTER	Nowt lasts
HUNTER	Perhaps William Hunter will always be the boy from North Shiel-eds
HUNTER	I keep telling you, I'm not a boy!
CLAUD	Perhaps I was wrong. Perhaps it is your soldiers you need, your war
HUNTER	I don't need that lot, I -
CLAUD	Perhaps you go back to your killing
HUNTER	It's not like that, it's -

CLAUD Look at me. Look at me! (HE DOES SO) Only one time William Hunter. One time. You understand?

HUNTER Bloody hell....

CLAUD Now, I cry. Now I am all in little pieces (EXIT CLAUDETTE)

SCENE FOURTEEN
(BACK AT CAMP NEXT DAY. ALL SOLDIERS PRESENT. SMILEY IS IN STATE OF SOME DISTRESS. ENTER SERGEANT WHO STEADIES HIMSELF)

SERGE Right, you ignorant load of bastards. A bit of news for you all.. We go over the top at dusk.

WHITE Yeah!

HUNTER You mean – today?

SERGE Well, we could always put it back a week or two if the present arrangement is not convenient for you, Hunter. (SHOUTS) Yes, you stupid Geordie bastard, today!

HUNTER But I thought we weren't going till –

SERGE This is the British Army, Hunter. Don't try to think. Any questions? (BEAT) You alright, Private Smiley?

WHITE I'll sort Smiley out, don't you worry Serge

SERGE See that you do. I've had my fill of poncy prats. Ready within the hour. (EXITS)

HUNTER What do I do, Stevens?

STEVE Do?

HUNTER   I've met this woman, Claudette

WHITE   Oh, he got his end away did he, the randy Geordie?
             (HUNTER MOVES STEVENS AWAY FROM THE
             OTHER TWO)

HUNTER   I can't stop thinking about her

STEVENS   Oh yeah?

HUNTER   Nothing happened. Well, everything did, in a way

WHITE   (SHOUTS OVER) He's making it all up, Stevens. Bet
             he never even got a feel!

HUNTER   But I screwed up

STEVENS   This woman's really got to you

HUNTER   We only love once in life. That's what she said

STEVENS   She might be right

HUNTER   Just the one chance

STEVENS   And you think this is it?

HUNTER   Dunno. But I screwed up anyway

STEVENS   And?

HUNTER   She cried, She cried for me, Stevens. Then she left.
             I've got to go back. Now

STEVENS   Now? But we go over the top

HUNTER   I know. What do I do?

STEVENS   Why not go tomorrow?

HUNTER   Too late.

STEVENS   You know what you're saying?

HUNTER   You're the poet. You tell me.

STEVENS   You're talking desertion

HUNTER   What's any of this crap out here to do with me anyway? I don't even know what I'm fighting for. Just want to see Claudette. How can I just pick up the rifle and start firing?

WHITE   (COMES OVER AND INTERRUPTS) Who was it then, Hunter? Some fat old scrubber? She'll probably give you the pox. (HUNTER NUTS HIM. HE FALLS. SLOWLY GETS TO HIS FEET) You'll regret that, you Geordie bastard

HUNTER   Don't say another word to me. Ever.

WHITE   He's broken my sodding nose

STEVENS   You're alright. It'll just bleed for a while.

HUNTER   Tell me it's alright, Stevens

STEVENS   Alright?

HUNTER   How can I do it? Just pick up that gun? Walk up that ladder?

STEVENS   You realise the alternative?

HUNTER   How can I do that? Walk away from Claudette, and everything I want?

STEVENS   (QUOTES)*"Sooner murder an infant in its cradle, than nurse unacted desires."*

HUNTER   What's that?

STEVENS   It's William Blake

HUNTER   Who?

STEVENS   William Blake. A visionary poet

HUNTER   Say it again

STEVENS   *"Sooner murder an infant in its cradle, than nurse unacted desires."*

HUNTER   What am I doing here, Stevens?

STEVENS   Get yourself away, Hunter. Before the roll call. I'll do my best to cover for you as long as I can. But don't come back. Not ever. Leave all of this, both of you

WHITE   Am I hearing this right?

STEVENS   Yeah

WHITE   You're putting yourself in the shit. Look at my nose? I thought you were alright Stevens.

             (ENTER SERGE)

SERGE   Right you lot, all present and correct? (CHECKS THEM OUT) Where's Hunter? (SILENCE) Well?

STEVE   I believe he might be sick, Sergeant

SERGE   Sick?

STEVE   He might be, yes, Sergeant

SERGE   Reported to the M.O, has he? (SILENCE) Well?

STEVE   Not sure Sergeant, but -

SERGE   Not sure? The poet's not sure? You covering something up, Stevens?

WHITE   He's off shagging, Sergeant

SERGE   What's that?

WHITE   Hunter. He attacked me then went off shagging some bit of French stuff, Serge

SERGE   (COMES CLOSE UP TO HIM) What are you saying, Private White?

WHITE   Bragging about it, he was, Serge. Getting his leg over with some French woman. Probably a married woman, too. I pity the husband

SERGE   The husband?

WHITE   Hunter doesn't give a shite for such things, if you don't mind me saying so. You alright, Sergeant?

SERGE   (RECOVERS) Runner! (ENTER RUNNER) I want two men sent to the village. Find Private William Hunter, and arrest him for desertion. Put him under lock and key (WHISTLE SOUNDS. THEY START TO GO OVER THE TOP. WE HAVE LIGHT AND SOUND OF BATTLE)

SCENE FIFTEEN
(HUNTER RUNS INTO THE VILLAGE . CLAUDETTE ENTERS FROM OTHER SIDE)

CLAUD   You came back

HUNTER   I had to

CLAUD   Yes

HUNTER	Sorry – a bit scruffy....I mean....I was in a hurry, no time to -
CLAUD	A hurry?
HUNTER	Yeah. .....I feel kinda
CLAUD	What?
HUNTER	Light-headed. I could just take off – like one of them observation balloons. Whoosh!
CLAUD	Whoosh?
HUNTER	Up in the air – whoosh!
CLAUD	Ah – whoosh! I go 'whoosh' with you
BOTH	Whoosh!
HUNTER	Can I just –
CLAUD	What?
HUNTER	I just want to touch your arm. (DOES SO). Look, I'm a bit – er -
CLAUD	What?
HUNTER	Lousy. Lice. On the body. Crawling. Hard to get rid of. Sorry
CLAUD	Lousy does not matter. Coming back. That matters
HUNTER	Aye. It does
CLAUD	More important than lousy
HUNTER	Aye. More important than –

CLAUD   Than anything

HUNTER   Your arm's soft. Everything where I am is hard, brittle

CLAUD   And you?

HUNTER   You have to be hard. To survive

CLAUD   Ah

HUNTER   (CONTINUES STROKING) Your flesh isn't hard

CLAUD   And my flesh survives

HUNTER   You were right, Claudette (BEAT). About everything. It's like I just woke up. All I can think about is you. The rest, all that out there, it's –

CLAUD   Yes?

HUNTER   It's all pretend, that's what it is. Only this makes sense. Like a bloody great flash, it was. Like one of them maroons. Bloody hell. Claudette, I think I love you. (PAUSE) Did you hear me?

CLAUD   Yes. I heard

HUNTER   Never said that seriously before

CLAUD   You cannot say it unless you are serious

HUNTER   Yeah. But you know what women are like– always asking if you love them
CLAUD   People must never ask. Only say

HUNTER   Well they asked (MIMICS) 'Do you love me Billy? 'Say you love me, Billy!' Whey aye, I'd say

CLAUD   (MIMICS) Whey aye

HUNTER   Hey, not bad! We'll make a Geordie of you yet! Mebbes you were right. Mebbes we only love once

CLAUD   Yes. Only once

HUNTER   So this is it – for me?

CLAUD   For me as well

HUNTER   Shit

CLAUD   It is simple. William Hunter of North Shiel-eds. I love you (SOUND OF GUNS) Where are the soldiers?

HUNTER   How do you mean?

CLAUD   Your other soldiers, there are none in the village

HUNTER   They've gone over the top

CLAUD   Into battle?

HUNTER   Aye

CLAUD   And you came to see me?

HUNTER   I had to

CLAUD   You will be in trouble

HUNTER   Mebbes

CLAUD   You disobey orders?

HUNTER   They're just bloody orders, man

CLAUD   This could be bad for you, William Hunter. Bad for us

HUNTER   Me mate Stevens will try and cover for me

CLAUD   I am afraid now

HUNTER   You didn't want to see me, then?

CLAUD   Always I want to see you

HUNTER   There you are then

CLAUD   But they will come for you

HUNTER   And I've come for you. You can say tara to this place Claudette. We both can

CLAUD   I must hide you, now!

HUNTER   Hide me?

CLAUD   They will be looking. Very soon

HUNTER   I love you Claudette

CLAUD   Please William Hunter. I must not lose you

HUNTER   You'll never lose me, pet.

CLAUD   I find somewhere safe to hide you. Then later, when it is dark, we leave

HUNTER   Aye. A new life!

CLAUD   (MAKES TO GO. HUNTER PULLS HER BACK. KISSES HER. DURING THE KISS, ENTER TWO SOLDIERS)

SOLDIER   Private William Hunter. Loyal North Lancs Regiment – you are under arrest for desertion! (THEY TAKE HIM OFF)

SCENE SIXTEEN
(BARRETT, DEFENDING OFFICER COMES TO
SEE HUNTER)

BARR   The name is Captain Barrett, Hunter. I've been chosen as your Prisoner's Friend

HUNTER   Friend?

BARR   Your defending counsel in the coming Court Martial

HUNTER   Right. You one of them barristers or solicitors or something?

BARR   I am simply an army officer

HUNTER   But you've trained in this kind of thing?

BARR   Not really, no

HUNTER   You've done it before though?

BARR   This is the first time I've been asked

HUNTER   Great.

BARR   So Hunter. Why exactly did you desert your post?

HUNTER   The thing is, I was underage when I signed up

BARR   What?

HUNTER   When I signed up, I was only seventeen

BARR   You lied about your age when you signed up?

HUNTER   Loads of blokes did. Some of them were hardly out of short trousers. No bugger cared

BARR   Do you have your birth certificate?

HUNTER   Oh aye. I carry it everywhere

BARR   This is a serious matter, Hunter

HUNTER   For who?

BARR   No birth certificate then. And why exactly did you
             sign up underage?

HUNTER   Why do you think?

BARR   Because you felt a burning and irresistible desire to
             fight for your beloved country?

HUNTER   I had the chance of a screw

BARR   To continue; I assume that you still feel that same
             burning and irresistible desire to fight for your
             beloved country, despite this unfortunate lapse.
             Which is why I need to know, just why did you desert
             your post?

HUNTER   I fell in love with a French girl

BARR   You deserted for a woman?

HUNT   I fell in love, see? You ever been in love?

BARR   This woman you met -

HUNTER   Claudette

BARR   Do you wish to tell me anything about this – this
             Claudette

HUNTER   Like what?

BARR   Let's try this, shall we? she took advantage of you,
             got you drunk, made you forget to return to your
             platoon, for which you are now truly repentant

HUNTER   Nah

BARR   Right (WRITES) *Temporary infatuation, possibly
            due to age.* You are actually underage I assume
            Hunter? You're not merely claiming to be so to
            improve your chances of escaping the death penalty?

HUNTER   Nobody wants to die, man

BARR   You're not making this easy for me

HUNTER   Not that easy for me mate, either

BARR   I may be the one person to stand between you and a
            firing squad

HUNTER   Just tell them I was underage. They don't bloody well
            know any different

BARR   I would feel much happier with a defence built round
            a young man inadvertently led astray, a temporary
            blip for which he is now truly repentant.

HUNTER   That's a load of bollocks

BARR   Are you taking this seriously, Hunter?

HUNTER   Can you not see, man? I'm shit scared. I want to live.
            Want to be with Claudette. They don't shoot soldiers
            who sign up underage.

BARR   As a rule, that is correct. But desertion is a capital
            offence and taken very seriously by the British Army

HUNTER   I don't give a toss about the British Army

BARR   I suggest we don't use that line of response during
            your court-martial

HUNTER   It's up to you

BARR   Do you intend to return to your duties as a loyal
                    soldier once you have served whatever punishment is
                    considered satisfactory?

HUNTER   Going back?

BARR   The court will expect some manifestation of
                    future loyalty

HUNTER   You expect me to get up and say all that rubbish?

BARR   I'm finding this difficult, Hunter. Claiming to have
                    fallen in love will cut little ice with the officers of the
                    Court Martial

HUNTER   I'm not lying about Claudette. Not to nobody. Just
                    tell them I was underage, man. If it helps, I'll not
                    even speak. Best way. I'm not lying about Claudette

BARR   You're probably right. I think our job is made easier
                    if you don't speak. I'll speak on your behalf.(STARTS
                    WRITING) Why don't we try something like this? A
                    compromise. It will be your own statement, read in
                    court by myself (GIVES IT HIM. HUNTER READS)

HUNTER   *Now I realise I have played the fool all along. I ask*
                    the court to be lenient with me. I am young and
                    have always been easily led. During this time I got
                    in league with a young woman and did not like
                    to leave her. I am not afraid of the trenches and if
                    leniently treated this time I hope to make a good
                    soldier. Some of that's true. The part that says I'm
                    young. And that I did not like to leave her

BARR   I suggest this is the best we can do if you wish to
                    save your life. I must warn you the sentence would
                    still be severe

HUNTER   Severe?

BARR   Hard labour, that kind of thing.Sign along the
      bottom line please (HUNTER SIGNS)

HUNTER I need to see Claudette again

BARR   I'm afraid there's absolutely no chance of that. I shall
      return tomorrow. Guard! (HE IS LET OUT)

HUNTER No chance of that, eh? We'll see (MAKES NOISES
      OF PAIN AND LIES CURLED IN A CORNER.
      GUARD COMES IN AND APPROACHES. HUNTER
      OVERPOWERS HIM AND ESCAPES. GUARD
      RAISES ALARM)

GUARD   Prisoner escaped! Prisoner escaped!

SCENE SEVENTEEN
      (HUNTER IS ON THE RUN, SOLDIERS ARE
      AFTER HIM, CLAUDETTE IS REACHING OUT TO
      HIM TO NO AVAIL. EVENTUALLY HE REACHES
      HER BUT AS HE GOES TO EMBRACE HER
      SOLDIERS ARE THERE TO RE-ARREST HIM.
      HUNTER AND CLAUDETTE ALMOST TOUCH BUT
      NOT QUITE)

SCENE EIGHTEEN
      (BARRATT AND SERGEANT)

BARR   If I may say so, Sergeant, you do not seem to be
      treating my role as Hunter's defending counsel with
      the respect it deserves

SERGE   I'm sure you'll do your best. Sir

BARR   Hunter claims he enlisted underage. Any comment?

SERGE   They'd say anything, Captain

BARR   Do you have any reason to doubt that claim?

SERGE   No more than you do to accept it. This is war. No-one
           has time to check birth records. Or much else

BARR   The British Army policy is not to shoot men who
           signed up underage, you know that, Sergeant?

SERGE   I know all of British Army policy. Sir. But Desertion
           is desertion in my book

BARR   You don't particularly like Hunter, do you
           sergeant?

SERGE   I'm a professional soldier, Captain. Not my job to like
           or dislike the snivelling wretch

BARR   Is he a good soldier?

SERGE   Private Hunter is not a good soldier, no sir

BARR   In what way?

SERGE   Insubordinate. Undisciplined. He treats the British
           Army and all it stands for with disrespect

BARR   Not just a soldier's normal healthy cynicism about
           authority?

SERGE   More than that, sir

BARR   There does seem some doubt about his age, and he
           is probably a young man easily led. It seems to me
           the British Army is capable of viewing this one lapse
           with a certain charity and we could recommend an
           alternative sentence. Possibly a spell in prison with
           hard labour. What do you think?

SERGE   Hunter is guilty of desertion, thereby putting in
           danger the lives of his fellow soldiers. And desertion
           for the most base and unworthy of reasons. On top
           of which, he then escaped custody to desert a second

time. Let soldiers get away with this kind of thing and what's left? Or maybe you hadn't thought about that. Sir

BARR   I think I get the picture sergeant. Thank you (EXIT SERGEANT)

SERGE   Someone has to get the picture. If this war's to count for anything (WRITES LETTER). *Dear Field Marshall Haig. Please excuse this unofficial method of communication from a humble Platoon Sergeant. May God and our country strengthen your valiant efforts. I believe yours is the final decision on Private William Hunter of the Loyal North Lancs Regiment. I am the man's platoon sergeant. Firstly General, I do not believe Hunter was underage when he signed up. Neither do I believe someone who puts the lives of his fellow soldiers at risk to indulge carnal desire is worth a reprieve.To reprieve this man would bring the army into disrepute at a time when maximum discipline is required. Can I strongly recommend that a sentence of execution be carried out. Thank you for taking the time and consideration to read this letter.* Runner! (RUNNER COMES ON AND TAKES LETTER)

SCENE NINETEEN
     (JUDGEMENT IS PASSED ON HUNTER BY THE COURT. TRENCH IS RECREATED AS SERGE WAITS FOR THE VERDICT)

JUDGEM.   No. 10710, Private William Hunter. You have been found guilty by this Court Martial that when on active service you did desert your post. Further, that when in confinement, you did escape. The penalty for such an offence is to suffer death by being shot. The court strongly recommends to mercy on the grounds of extreme youth, service in the field and likelihood of being a good fighting man.

WILSON   I think the man ought to be shot, except he is very
              young. I recommend that the sentence be commuted
              to five years penal servitude. Not to be suspended.
              Lieutenant General Henry Wilson

SANDERSON   His character as a fighting man is nil as he intends to
              do no fighting. Lt Colonel M. Sanderson

HOLLAND   I am of the opinion that the death sentence should be
              inflicted. He is no good as a fighting soldier.
              Major General A. Holland
              (BARRETT ENTERS AND HANDS VERDICT
              TO SERGE)

SCENE TWENTY

SERGE   It looks like we'll be saying goodbye to Private
              Hunter at dawn tomorrow

STEVE   The firing squad?

SERGE   Right first time, Private Stevens. Answer your names
              when called. Private Smiley (NO RESPONSE)
              Private Smiley?

STEVENS   I don't think Smiley is well, Sergeant

SERGE   I see no injuries

STEVENS   It's more psychological. They call it shell shock

SERGE   I've heard of this so-called 'shell shock'

STEVENS   According a recent article by Charles Myers in
              The Lancet -

SERGE   You bloody what?

STEVENS   That article claims –

SERGE   What some poncy article claims, Stevens, doesn't count for a sparrow's arsehole out here. Any half-baked cowardly soldier afraid of fighting the enemy is hiding behind this so-called 'shell-shock'. Private Smiley. Look at me. Look at me. You are a soldier in the British Army, Smiley. And that's what you're proud to be. You are commanded to form part of the firing squad to carry out the execution of Private William Hunter, a soldier shown to be in gross dereliction of duty, thereby putting his fellow soldiers at risk. (SMILEY STARTS CRYING)

SMILEY   No, no, no. no, I .....

SERGE   Pull yourself together, you pathetic individual

STEVE   Sergeant, I really think –

SERGE   Shut it Stevens

SERGE   Now listen Smiley (TAKES HIM TO ONE SIDE). I understand you may have had a part to play in the disappearance of Private White's gas mask

SMILEY   M-m-m-Mask

SERGE   A serious offence likely to result in the innocent and painful death of a British soldier

SMILEY   M-m-m-mask? –

SERGE   I am in my rights to order a court of enquiry into the same disgraceful incident

SMILEY   I – I -

SERGE   You understand the potential severity of such a court of enquiry?

SMILEY   Mmmmm -

SERGE	A capital offence. However, I am prepared to show some leniency in this matter, given the right circumstances. Now, I want you to be a good boy, pull yourself together and get on with the job of being a soldier. You understand?
SMILEY	I – I – (LOOKS TO STEVENS)
STEVE	Serge, I really think –
SERGE	I told you - stay out of this, poet. I want you to be in that firing squad tomorrow Private Smiley. I want Hunter to see exactly who is lining up to shoot him. You got that?
STEVE	Now look here Serge, Smiley's unbalanced, he's –
SERGE	He's a bloody simpering nutcase that's what he is. And about as much use to the British Army as wet toast. But he's going to be there, like the rest of you
STEVE	But giving him a live rifle in his unstable state, he could fire anywhere and –
SERGE	Private Smiley gets the blank. I'll make sure of that. Got it? He can aim where he bloody well likes But he will be part of that firing squad. And Hunter will see him. The last thing he does see. Pull yourself together now Smiley! (ROUGHS HIM UP A BIT THROUGH ALL THIS). Attention Private Smiley! I said attention! (EVENTUALLY COMES TO ATTENTION) Not a game out here lad, not for the squeamish. But you'll be there tomorrow and you'll thank your platoon sergeant for selecting you, won't you? I said *won't you*!
SMILEY	Y- yes, Sergeant
SERGE	Thanks him then. Thank him properly

SMILEY   Th- thank you, sergeant

SERGE   Good. At ease Private Smiley.
Now, Private Stevens.....

STEVE   This is barbaric. Permission to be excused, Sergeant

SERGE   Say that again, Private Stevens

STEVE   Permission to be excused partaking in the firing squad, Sergeant

SERGE   Reasons?

STEVE   I feel a moral repugnance at the concept of shooting in cold blood. one of our own soldiers who is also a friend, Sergeant. This is a level of barbarity to which no civilised army or nation should sink. We have no right to any claim to be a civilised society when we indulge in such acts of primitive retribution - Sergeant

SERGE   Well, Private Stevens, why don't we just let our soldiers do what they like, eh? When we say it's time to attack, why not let them scive off with some loose French tart if they want to? They may, in their own little way, reduce the chances of our winning this war against a cruel and pitiless enemy, but where's the harm in that, eh?

STEVE   I formally request that my place in the firing squad be taken by another soldier, sergeant

SERGE   A word, Private. (TAKES HIM ASIDE) You wouldn't be feeling guilty at all, Private Stevens, would you?

STEVE   Guilty, Sergeant?

SERGE   I believe you encouraged Hunter to desert and commit carnal acts. Well?

STEVE   I – I -

SERGE   And then attempted to cover up this most
            appalling of crimes. I may well find myself with no
            alternative other than to take into account your own
            contribution in this act of desertion.

STEVE   Contribution, Sergeant?

SERGE   Let me spell it out for you, poet. Just so you and
            your poetry don't go putting any more hairbrained
            ideas into the minds of serving soldiers in the British
            Army. The act of desertion is viewed so seriously by
            the British Army that it carries the ultimate penalty
            of death by firing squad. This same penalty would
            apply to anyone found both assisting this act of
            desertion and/or attempting to cover it up. Should
            you fully co-operate in the army's judicial system,
            then I may find it a way to overlook your own crimes.
            If not......Well? (PAUSE). The poet has nothing to
            say. I assume silence implies consent. Good. Where
            is Private White? Private White! (ENTER WHITE)
            Private White, you have been selected to form part
            of tomorrow's dawn firing squad for Private William
            Hunter

WHITE   Thank you Serge. Thank you very much Serge! I
            consider it an honour

SERGE   At ease, everyone! (EXIT SERGE TRENCH
            TRANSFORMS INTO HUNTER'S HOME)

SCENE TWENTY ONE
            (MARGARET IS AT HOME. A KNOCK TO THE
            DOOR. SHE ANSWERS IT. IT IS STEVENS WITH A
            SMALL CARDBOARD BOX)

STEVE   Mrs. Hunter?

MARG   Yes?

STEVE   My name's Henry Stevens, Mrs.Hunter. I was in the
               same regiment as your son, William. I bought a few
               of his things along

MARG   You'd better come in, Mr. Stevens

STEVE   Thank you (ENTERS) I'll not stay, I -. (HANDS
               OVER BOX)

MARG   Thank you (LOOKS IN BOX)

STEVE   Well, I'll – (MAKES TO GO)

MARG   Don't go just yet Mr Stevens. I'll put the kettle on.
               I'm sure you could do with a cuppa. I'm sorry my
               husband's not at home. Have you come far?

STEVE   From Liverpool. I'm on leave. From the Western
               front. I'm very very sorry about your son, Mrs
               Hunter. Just thought you might like those few things

MARG   That's very kind of you Mr. Stevens. You were his
               friend?
STEVE   I think I was, yes

MARG   You were probably a good friend to our William,
               Mr. Stevens

STEVE   Out there in the trenches, you value your friends

MARG   (SELECTS) William's watch – it never kept good
               time! (SELECTS) My letters – he never replied
               much (READS AND QUOTES) *'My Dear Son, it is
               now five weeks since I heard from you last and it
               makes us very anxious, although......'* (BREAKS OFF.
               REPLACES LETTER IN BOX.PUTS BOX DOWN).
               I'll look at those later, Mr Stevens

STEVE   Yes, yes, of course

MARG   I never really understood why William signed up.
              It's not as if he cared about things like that. People
              waving flags and all

STEVE   I suppose he had his reasons

MARG   He never said much. In the few letters he did send

STEVE   Not always easy, writing letters out there

MARG   I suppose not

STEVE   Look - I don't think I'll stay for that tea if it's all the
              same. I just wanted to bring you the box and -

MARG   Nothing's very easy, is it?

STEVE   No, no, of course not. Well, I –

MARG   Don't go yet, Mr. Stevens

STEVE   What?

MARG   Don't go

STEVE   Well, I should really and -

MARG   How did William die?

STEVE   What?

MARG   How did he die, Mr. Stevens

STEVE   What do you mean?

MARG   Well, how did my son die?

STEVE   Well - what did the army tell you?

MARG   They just sent me this. (GETS LETTER. GIVES
            IT HIM)

STEVENS   (READS) *'We regret to inform you that your son
            Private William Hunter has been killed on active
            service'* That's everything?

MARG   Yes

STEVE   I see

MARG   A mother needs more than that, if she's to have peace
            of mind. I've made enquiries – got me nowhere. So
            how was my son killed Mr. Stevens? Was he shot? An
            explosion? Did he die right away or in hospital? Did
            he suffer?

STEVE   He didn't suffer, no

MARG   Well? How? (PAUSE) How did my son die,
            Mr. Stevens

STEVE   Look, I - (MAKES TO GO)

MARG   How?

STEVE   He was shot

MARG   How was he shot?

STEVE   Just shot

MARG   What, a stray bullet? Machine gun?

STEVE   He was – shot at dawn

MARG   Shot at Dawn?

STEVE   Yes

MARG   You mean, a firing squad?

STEVE   Yes

MARG   Why was my son shot?

STEVE   Look, Mrs Stevens, I –

MARG   Why was my son shot, Mr Stevens?

STEVE   Desertion

MARG   He deserted? William?

STEVE   Yes (ENTER BELLA)

BELLA   Mrs. Hunter, I just thought I'd -

MARG   Mr. Stevens, This is Bella. Bella and William, they were – that is, she was hoping, when he eventually returned –

BELLA   What is it Mrs. Hunter? Why is Mr Stevens here?

MARG   He came to tell us about William. William was shot at dawn Bella. He deserted his post. So they shot him. A firing squad. Why did my son desert Mr. Stevens? He was not a coward, whatever else he was. (BEAT) I have to know Mr. Stevens. We both do

STEVE   I'm not sure I –

MARG   You've come a long way Mr. Stevens. Too far not to tell the truth. Why did my son desert?

STEVE   There was – a woman

BELLA   A woman? What do you mean, a woman? Are you saying Billy deserted for a woman?

STEVE Out there. It's not like here. People do all sorts of things – strange things, they -

BELLA He left his post and his fellow soldiers for a woman?

STEVE Yes

BELLA He wouldn't do that. Not Billy. Would he, Mrs. Hunter? Not Billy.What sort of a woman? I mean, what was her name? What did she look like? A French woman? Was she – (MARGARET RESTRAINS HER)

MARG Who was in this firing squad Mr. Stevens? Who killed my son?

STEVE I'd rather not say any more, I –

MARG You can't just leave it at that. Not now. Who killed my son?

STEVE Soldiers

MARG What soldiers?

STEVE Just – soldiers

MARG Where did they come from, these soldiers?

STEVE The platoon

MARG My son's platoon?

STEVE That's right, Mrs Hunter

MARG Your platoon?

STEVE Yes

MARG Were you one of the soldiers who shot my son?

STEVE   Yes

BELLA   You killed Billy? (SILENCE)

MARG   You aimed a rifle at my son's heart and pulled the trigger?

STEVE   Yes

MARG   Why did you come here, Mr. Stevens?

STEVE   I don't know, I –

MARG   You've done no good by coming here, you understand that?

STEVE   I just thought –

MARG   You've broken two women's hearts by coming here

STEVE   I don't know – I wanted to –that is, I thought –

BELLA   Billy – another woman? And you shot him?

(MARGARET COMFORTS HER)

MARG   You'd best go Mr. Stevens. I think you've done everything you can do here

STEVE   I'm really sorry, I –

MARG   Just go. (HE MAKES TO GO. STOPS BY THE DOOR. BEAT)

BELLA   Mr. Stevens?

STEVE   Yes?

BELLA   Where have you come from today?

STEVE   From Liverpool .

BELLA   That's a long journey

STEVE   Not really, I –

BELLA   We should both thank you for coming Mr. Stevens.
              You meant well. And it can't have been easy for you

STEVE   I just wanted to bring a few things and -

BELLA   You could have not come at all. You could have not
              told us the truth. Either would have been easier

STEVE   Yes

BELLA   Mrs. Hunter's right. You have broken two women's
              hearts. But that's not your fault. That's the trouble
              with the truth sometimes. It's not very – very
              comfortable

STEVE   No, I know

BELLA   Perhaps you'll come and see us again some time.
              When all this is over (LOOKS AT MARGARET
              WHO ASSENTS)

STEVE   Perhaps

BELLA   I think you need to go now

STEVE   Yes. Goodbye Bella. Goodbye Mrs. Hunter
              (EXIT STEVENS.)

SCENE TWENTY TWO

(THE FIRING SQUAD LOCATION. DRUMS. STAKE
IN THE GROUND. HUNTER IS BROUGHT ON BY
TWO SOLDIERS. ENTER SERGEANT, STEVENS,
WHITE, SMILEY AND REST OF FIRING SQUAD.
AFTER HUNTER IS ALLOWED TO SEE THEM HE
IS BLINDFOLDED)

SERGE   Firing squad – formation!(COME TO FORMATION)
Firing squad - attention (COME TO ATTENTION).
Firing squad – one step forward! (DO SO)

STEVE   Forgive me, Hunter

SERGE   Firing squad – present arms! (DO SO)

STEVE   Forgive me

SERGE   Firing squad – take aim (DO SO)

WHITE   He had his fun. And he left the rest of us in the shit

(SERGEANT NOW TAKES OUT WHITE
HANDKERCHIEF WHICH HE HOLDS UP.
SERGEANT BRINGS DOWN THE WHITE
HANDKERCHIEF. THE SQUAD FIRES)

END OF PLAY

CLOUD NINE THEATRE COMPANY was created in 1997 and remains true to its founding principle of only performing new writing and only by northern writers. No classics, Shakespeare or adaptations. It still lives in Cullercoats, where it was born.

In recent years it has established a regular small-scale venue at *The Low Lights Tavern*, North Shields and since early 2012 has premiered ten separate shows there.

The programme is linked to a series of play writing workshops which seek to nurture the region's new writing talents and bring them to the stage.

If you'd like to be kept in touch with our future activities, do get in touch as below. Thank you!

cloudninetheatre@blueyonder.co.uk
www.cloudninetheatre.co.uk
0191-2531901

5 Marden Tce
Cullercoats
North Shields
NE30 4PD

Find us on Facebook and Twitter

PETER MORTIMER

PETER MORTIMER IS A POET, PLAYWRIGHT AND TRAVEL writer who has lived in the North East coastal village of Cullercoats since the mid-seventies. He enjoys the wide-open beaches and being buffeted by the constant winds.

He has written more than two dozen plays for various companies and more than a dozen of his books have singularly failed to storm the best-sellers charts. His latest book is *Made in Nottingham – a Writer's Return* (Five Leaves Publications) where he returned to live for a month on the street of his childhood on Sherwood council estate in Nottingham. He now plans a bizarre travel book involving random games of chess.

Peter is the founder/editor of IRON Press, artistic director of *Cloud Nine* and also set up the Shatila Theatre Project, working with young Palestinian refugees in Lebanon. His grandfather, Alex Mortimer, served in the trenches on the western front.

www.petermortimer.co.uk

NEIL ARMSTRONG

NEIL HAS DIRECTED MANY A SHOW FOR *CLOUD NINE*. HE'S actually lost count of how many he's done since he first worked for the company back in the late 1990s but productions include *The Selkie* by Valerie Laws, *Influence* by Paul Buie, *The Battling Ettricks* by Mary Pickin, as well as a host of Peter Mortimer plays such as *She's on Toast, Clockman, A Parcel for Mr.Smith* and *The Stolen Rubber Band*. Neil said, "I love working for *Cloud Nine*, you end up in some wonderful places both mentally and physically. Over the years we've staged shows in not only theatres but also in pubs, hotels, community centres, yoga centres, working-men's clubs, football clubs and on one memorable occasion we performed on the platform of Whitley Bay Metro Station. Never a dull moment and long may it continue."

Neil has also directed productions for The Customs House South Shields, Live Theatre Newcastle, Theatre of Moths, The Gala Theatre Durham and Newcastle Theatre Royal. Also a writer, Neil's last play *Remember Jim* won best show at the Sunderland Cultural awards and his latest play *The End of the Pier* will be produced by *Cloud Nine* and go on tour in the summer of 2016.

Cloud Nine would like to thank the following North East organisations for their generosity in sponsoring individual performances of the 2016 production of *Death at Dawn:*

Read Milburn Accountants, North Shields

Key Enterprises (1983) Limited

EastCoast Taxis & Tyne Idol Tours

ENGIE (GDF Suez)

Lightning Source UK Ltd.
Milton Keynes UK
UKOW06f2125150216

268418UK00008B/90/P